THE CONCRETE GARDEN

THE
CONCRETE
GARDEN

G.F. DUTTON

BLOODAXE BOOKS

ISBN: 1 85224 141 1

First published 1991 by
Bloodaxe Books Ltd,
P.O. Box 1SN,
Newcastle upon Tyne NE99 1SN.

Bloodaxe Books Ltd acknowledges
the financial assistance of Northern Arts.

Cover reproduction by V & H Reprographics, Newcastle upon Tyne.

Printed in Great Britain by
Bell & Bain Limited, Glasgow, Scotland.

*The fragility of the flower
unbruised
penetrates space*

WILLIAM CARLOS WILLIAMS

Acknowledgements

Acknowledgements are due to the editors of the following publications in which most of these poems – or their prototypes – first appeared: *Akros, AMF, Chapman, InFolio, Lines Review, New Writing Scotland* (5, 7 & 8), *Northlight, Poetry Wales, Smoke, Verse* and *Words*.

Contents

A Pointed Spade

You need a pointed spade
for ground like this.

To be of use
in this last rock and turf.

A square-edged blade
so good to double-trench

that first allotment
would be bent

never penetrate
this kind of earth.

You need to wrench
then drive it straight

lever to and fro
spoon up the stones

deep as you can go.
An inch or two to start

then once you're in,
no doubt.

But time, and finding soil to fill
the hole you've lifted out.

Culture

Just to choose
a corner of the wilderness
is to enclose

it with intent.
Is to create
garden, gardener

a life spent
cropping the rubble, a desire
to regulate

what goes by,
catch at a scent, ensure
some branch against the sky.

Is to incur
from the first day
what creation cost, the haste

to cut and tear,
rake things over.
At the least the need

to look about, decide
what wild flower
is now a weed.

Docken

And there is a docken
that each year
grows hugely in a corner
of the carpark, that has seen

three factories take on this site
and has outlived
all three, survived to be
just now Japanese, it is

a great favourite,
old Willie Stout
the gardener does not dare
spray it or howk it out.

A tall docken
with a long stem
that rises from
the secret to the sun.

Flat

Like much of Scotland
this is a flat land,
stretched between

mountains and shore
grey cloud grey haar
most of the year

and has been
no doubt
often as flat

though shrugged about
various seas,
dipped and raised

time again,
kindled, braised
iced to the bone;

nevertheless,
smoothed with pale green
under a weak sun

and offered to
shall we say man,
it had its attractions.

Whether or no
any remain
or any new

have come in
is less certain.
These constructions

dot it sadly, though
big at the feet,
for this is not

climate for concrete,
and mud
too rapidly succeeds

ideas of grass.
People and weeds
have to thrive here

roots and seeds
have to explore
momentary silt.

Have to cherish
leaf or even flower
of the one result.

Penalty

Natural
to play football
in a flat land

pointed and planned,
where streets invite
anguish at edges, wounds

from whatever surrounds.
Inevitable
some Saturday night

to come by a ball
that would bounce and roll
far on the flat

and to stop all that,
teach it drill,
trap it, keep it

spot-lit, still,
sized for a goal.
And only fair

to play it square,
even the score.
To kick by rule

strike that ball, net it while
cries rain down and
streamers fall

acknowledging out of the darkness.
They cheer us yet, gather about our
stamping and mismanaged feet.

Open to the Public

A machine
for walking in. All
gravel and stone

and strips of green
clipped and mown
beyond season, a non-

vegetation. And the steps
up and down, the seats –
who would sit on

marble, relax
so near the bone? Vistas,
terraces, who would not strut

staccattoing pavement, heel
such a rich
grind of gravel? Feet here

tread secure, they lead to
the centrepiece, the sculptor's
chiselled mistress

in her bowl; she spouts eyeball,
her fixed stare, re-
sistant musculature

distress the peace
of the Grand Parterre. The rest of the place
is so polite, so discreet.

Only when shut
is ever sprayed
with herbicide.

Campanula latifolia alba

is a tall
steeple of white bells
climbing, a carillon

with purple echoes
at the throat,
rooted

in a rosette
of devoted leaves.
All June

through the dry shadows
of open woodland
it grows

fast to the mind
and brought home
will grace estate

or plot. When petals are shed
and globes of green seed
hang silent below

the name will make do.
It is tied to the stem every season,
and tries to ring true.

Roses

That's what roses are for.
A rose is there
to keep you to the corner

so you go
where God's concrete
tells you to. No

sneaky-foot
short cut here,
a rose bush is razor-bare

it'll scare
you dead sober
you'll think twice

before you leave
the set truth
the public path. The public rose

blesses those
precast ways
with leaf and flower.

Should you dare
pick and choose
it drops all that

will bite and scratch
stab you at full stretch
in your own tracks.

A rose bush is
a coil of wire
that needs care

any night
to beat flat
pull right out.

You think of it
days after.
Each time you come to a corner.

Sabbath

The trees scream when they break them.
Such a passion
for destruction.

And a trail of earth
where the roots did not quite
come out,

all across the path.
It is Sunday morning
as it has been

often before and within the hour
doors will open,
every garden

receive a due
benediction. It is a day
if you live by the park

to seek peace, mark the observances,
clip hedges
against Gethsemane.

The Concrete Garden

It takes time
to become set. Before that

you spread it out
smack it, thrust

bright-eyed advances
about the agglomerate, sow

whatever is new,
is bound to grow,

push through
rise to you there – you

regarding from heaven
before the streets stiffen.

Even then, they swear, one mushroom
can break up a pavement.

Jihad

The road grips tighter
dives beneath
deep water

one bright path
beckoning miles
of tunnelling wheels, there are men

in every truck every car
they stare straight on
they will get there

they will be first it is a race
to break into Paradise,
it must burst

rise at the end
into some grand
acclamation of sun.

So many of them.
So able to drive
packed with explosive.

Hazard

A hazel tree
at the kerb of Seggie Way, survivor
of what was formerly

Seggie brae, alive here
by accident, decidedly
now no longer

permitted to stay. For
the road bends, it offends
blocks the view

of such a corner. And after
the earth mover
no sign

that it grew, a smooth green
safer distance, somewhat more
predictability. The cautious eye

ageless raviner
has picked the corner clean.
Can see

clearer than before
the end of the day.
The further difficulty in the sunset.

Serpentine

A kind of path
that won't pursue the truth
about a garden,

cannot square
with such severe
enclosure; but would rather

seek to please, gather
flowers, trees,
repeat the views

of every daily
dilly-dallier. It lies
so easy, is so busy

setting out
sequence of avoidance
through the green plot that

a shock to find
suddenly its end
bare wire. And

maybe an iron gate.
To go further,
you open that.

Faith

A bough fails,
the track's forsaken.
The tree falls
a house is broken.

Plant on;
chance has season.
This is autumn
without question.

Tall the oak,
rough its bark.
Its roots
consume silence.

Belief

This is their mountain,
a trodden disgrace.

The whole face rubble,
the track a struggle

stone to stone; each intention
slides back down. They need

a staircase laid, of regular tread,
to guide their feet

straight to the summit. But
they would cry out, never forgive

their elevation
interfered with,

made safe. They put weight
on the doubt.

A heap so rotten, you'd never believe
it could reach this height.

Ruins

We set three stones
together in the sand,
and rake them round.
They will reduce
the odds on emptiness

make us a place
to sit and meditate,
to gamble on the great
It-Might. Above the town,
along the beach,

rocks unassigned
randomly crouch,
cry for composition;
beseech us to guess
their anguish for order,

what might be gained
once they were tuned
by a single touch. But ruins –
ruins won't join in the play;
bids were too high

a previous day, their ashes
indicate loss, their wager
is over, they lie in despair
of raising another. They ask us
just to forget

the chance of an absolute.

Joy

Twenty-seven bullfinches
in one week
of sun

visited the blossom –
so sparse
now the years

close in – of my cherry trees
from Japan. They enjoyed
each opening bud

as much as I did, not
for the whiteness
not for food

but the delight
of ripping them out
and throwing them down, a circle of white

bleached the grass
under every tree. Pure
anarchy, sheer

destruction. There was something about them
misusing the sun
for private joy

that offended my sense
of our common inheritance. And must have been why
each day, I shot them.

Twenty-seven bullfinches
in one week of sun. The best,
almost, with that particular gun.

Interstadial

Once more that sand is extended
the glacier done, ended,
the blue snout the great ox-weight

emptied to silver and sunlight;
once more
that absence relaxes

before the return of the fuss.
Before moss
grass and the marching rootmat

before the rush
of the first forests, before
the first axes.

Mons Graupius

It is no
marching camp. Not for a day
those couples, those cables, the eagles

are here to stay.
It is a proposition
square in our way, come

bearing within it
the great street
that leads to Rome, and beyond

to whatever land
radiates an infinite.
We must go out

tomorrow and fight
for the sun's fortress
now they have brought us

the first road, measured
the first mile, now
we have understood Caesar.

Go down from the moon
take on the sun,
and all that comes after.

Nuclear Incident

The end of the road. And here
you may park a car, admire
the flowers, never

gather them. They bloom
too deep a green,
fierce a flame

their side the wire,
the fence, the fright
of notices keep out keep out. They are quite

impossible to pick, they stack
hectares with feverish
green and excitable yellow, thrive

brazenly alive, spray seeds
tomorrow. While clouds
come and go, the slow

earth unwinds, trees
beget trees and no
one really minds

no one will stop the bees. The wind blows
sweetly and reasonably
shades of any day across them.

Barbarians

To carry long spears
through a country of grass,

wind washing over
gold and silver,

is no new thing
has often been done,

will not shock the bog-cotton.
This is an empire

of grasses and air, far
from the engines of Caesar, it will endure

itch of the hand
another time round. And as for us,

though not of a mind
for deep ores, precise furnaces,

no loss; we understand
the white joy of platinum.

And follow the wind
with iron of our own.

Border

This is the Border,
like many another. An old wound

not yet healed, a fault
of geology maybe

or weather. Land
tossed about, crushed between

mist and rain, sleet and sun,
long brown

winding-on
summits of confusion. Ending in

the same black storm.
Nights heavy

with reconciliation
dawns clean

with the old bright treachery. And I
for life must stand

on this twice-turning roadway, lashed
by a two-faced wind and these

fierce roses that have climbed
down from each bank and rise entwined

before, about me
and behind.

Call

A furious wind
on the outer estates,
hail and sleet
at the high flats,

the street lights
flickering.
A good night
for visiting,

pillaging, trying
another's mind,
with something else
beating around

to think about,
to get in the talk.
Up at that door
two blocks back

held half-opened,
Jim and his wife,
his smile uneasy
hers the cool knife

sweet to remember.
Aye man come in,
Liz was just saying
you'd look along,

Christ what a bloody
hell of a wind.
He goes before me.
She behind.

After Brashing Pines

Brashing is
lopping off dead branches, old
entanglement, outgrown

gesture; so your trees
rise calm and clean into their own
September. When

you leave them, go home
they resume
high business, needle on needle

repeating, gathering
the night wind; and
you do not mind,

you do not look behind
at what's beginning again, what storm,
what growing collision of darkness.

You have no concern,
the job being done
and they putting up another season,

the tall leaders
quarrelling together
against their stars.

B

Weed Species

This is the tree
that grows straight, seed
of knowledge, planted, fed,
tended line by line to be

felled in a gale
of sawdust and petrol. Not those
over the fence, sown free,
broken by season, strays

swarming with eyes and evasion
pests and diseases, the wry
birch and aspen. Beautiful
weed species.

Crossing Over

Stones still grip
both banks, build up
squared assured

complete the arch; pledged
to centuries, old
ash roots, boulders, huge

shadows of pools. An obstinate
narrow bridge
cobbled and steep

it was replaced
by a simple flat
iron one, set between

two cubicular
precast abutments, well clear
of the nervous water; concrete

white, iron green, vanishing
either side
into the road unseen

by any driver. Proud
to make no fuss
crossing over.

Spate

Not a rock to be seen.
Last night the rain
washed snow black off and both
thrash white together down
this long roar of a glen. Children
dance on the bank, fling in
stones, old branches, scream
after scream. The river obeys them.
It takes everything away.

It is fast and powerful.
It has no hesitation.
It makes their day. They look so small,
they scream and strut
cocksurely
round and about.
They are the sole
and quite inaudible
great authors of this fury.

After

Not the sight of it
after the storm.
Not the oaks felled, their
tangle of branches, not
the sun through them
steaming the long roof-tree,
still firm.
But the breath held,
the great light of it,
and a silence the sound
of a horseman's hand
soothing repeatedly
some tremble of haunches.

Bridge

They watch the river passing through
however slow its oil and scum
because they know there is some place
it must go to,
it has come from.

And any river even this
out of the ever it journeys in
brings to their faces one by one
a time of their own
to reflect upon.

Beginner

A tractor and bogey
piled high
with baled hay,
in trouble
on this steep hill.

Such a noise
and no movement; until
blue smoke rises
wonderingly
above the gold.

Now he has got his gears in.
A great scold
of shacklepins, the conjunction
takes up again, rounds the
bad corner

for ever, the smoke and the noise
fade into trees. Cows
recompose
readjust to their grass.
Over

in less than a minute, before
how many million leaves of June.

Family Break

It is the first
full day of summer, skirts
of dizzy young trees

lift to a dead
breeze, they drop again
it is the June

holiday, it's why
this silence and the sad
road empty. Only one

packed Ford the last in town
blasts through the echoes, a child's arm
trails from its window, all rush on

to sky-high noon
brassed sun
leaves of leather. How soon has gone

white-shouldered dawn, that rare
just once together seen
imminence of summer.

Fracture

A very small table.
Not even a meal.

Just two glasses on it
both empty and I

am about to explain
there is wine in them still

when you smile and you lean
closer and closer and then

the table is over;
and both glasses broken.

No reason for guilt,
nobody's fault,

they are busy with cloths and apologies.
But you have destroyed my metaphor.

And I cannot take my eyes
from your eyes.

Weekend

Lights pick up,
lay aside,
as if for ever
pieces of road.

Wheels
banish them.
They are the same
ache of gravel

we walked upon.
That when we are gone
will come together,
making a dawn.

And us by then
asleep in some town.
Travelled how far,
as if to get nearer.

Issue

This is your ticket. Take it.
You can travel no hassle
air sea or land

or underground. Or sit an hour
maybe more
in some deckchair. Use it

to visit
gardens galleries
continents all that spite

of accumulation you
have a right
to the queue. When

you're done
it's handed in
or clipped and handed

back again, if you refuse
and stay at home
it's yours

it's issued just the same
you never win
or lose

the ticket game. Take out
your father's one best suit
he hardly left his room

slip in your hand
before behind
you find

empty pockets
stuffed with tickets.
Used and unused.

Waiting

Mist
has encompassed the city. About us
shocked forests

bleed into rust.
The airport lounge is crowded and hot
it can only repeat

delayed delayed. No one knows what
has shut itself off, uncoupled the breath, what is outside
whistling to silence. Myself and some woman beside me –

we have not spoken much
I have only seen her sideways
she has been knitting knitting children's jerseys–

wait for the crash; press
knees together des-
perately.

Carmen Mortis

Wha gangs alane
gangs free.

Wha's for companie,
gangs wi me.

Landfall

Rafted out on the darkness
we must agree

to think up a shore to sail to,
something other than sea.

We must appoint a captain
navigator and cook

disown the illusion of drowning
squat on the deck

row as if we remembered
count as hard as we can.

Till the black waves, numbered,
slip beneath us again

and night draws its conclusion
a single white line,

no visionary horizon
not even dawn.

But the raw edge of ocean
on rocks of iron.

The one destination
we agreed upon.

Dive

This is a dive.
The urge to within.
The reach to believe.
Try it. It will begin

dark, clamorous,
belabouring.
Weeds will implore you,
fishes and faces

beat at your head.
Ignore them.
You will heed
only what struggles to meet you,

the plain stare
of the sea floor, a square
of your own measure.
It will greet you

hug you with rarities,
sandgrain and stone
clutch of white shells.
Dismiss you again.

To sun at the surface, to pour
shell stone and sand
back through your hand
into indifferent water. Nor

anything more. That was your dive.
That was belief.
Being achieved
for the price of a breath.

Delegate

A mile off the crowded shore.
Not near. Not far.

Enough for a swim.
And to wave to them from,

to goggle their eyes
at the end of a glass.

They do not approve
my living above

such a deep underneath,
they mind

me treading on their drowned.
A mile off the crowded shore

rocking alone, about to postpone
tomorrow's midnight below.

Drawing a line
at what I will do.

I will float in the sun, nothing more,
lie as I am till the tide runs on,

shoulders me in
through darkening foam and the evening skerry.

Only a mile.
And today is no hurry.

All this I will tell them, and they will smile;
and towel my trembling body.

After the Swim

Up from the sea's rock –
you know the trick – fields
houses, look

a blue frock,
that child
regards you, holds

upside down its doll,
tries out a smile. You're halfway back,
follow the track

beyond, hard familiar ground,
you're going well, a whole school
plays football, through the noise

your last gull
cries and cries
with no voice. The land

you started out from, and the crowd
is cheering, on parade.
Knows nothing about you. Time

to pocket stone,
put on boots of iron,
walk across and join them.

Open Cast

It will all be put back
just as it was before.

At present, my dear,
it may be a scar
an open wound, a hole in the ground

a quarter mile square:
that's nothing to fear –
we have mended, all round,

holes that were,
filled them in by the million ton
hammered them down

to hectares of beautiful green, each one
rolled out between – how far, how far –
high-tensile wire;

and simply alive
with mutton and beef.
You'd never believe

how solid they are, how safe
with the ashes tucked underneath.
And this hole here

will be as pretty a place –
you'll recognise
the lane, the flowers, the trees

the field with the blue butterflies. And yes
you will love her as much as your mother, so please
don't cry any more.

It will all be put back
just as it was before.

Lachie

The roof lasted
a little longer than he did.
They sold his sheep, the beasts

went to the knackers, the tractor almost
too rusted
to move. He lived on

in drink and conversation,
guffaws, a hundred
tales of wit

and prowess fading slowly,
as the place itself had foundered
into one more green

nettle-making heap; but that
an architect bought it,
for weekend use,

with a professional wife
three small children
and a dog called Simon. Saturdays

from the hill the house
smokes at evening again,
fresh-painted, with a new straight roof.

They sold his sheep, the beasts
went to the knackers, the tractor almost
too difficult to move.

Death in October

Good to go off in colours.
Scarlet before the sleet;
fuming crimson, shrieking orange
a relaxed butter-pat

yellow. Name them. Anything
is better than flat
worn-out green. Even that
is strangely remote

in frost lying on the white
grass, whiter
edged, each vein
picked out for the last time, crystalline.

Pensioners

In various parts of the garden
you meet them,
the admirers
of flowers.

It is the colours
the freshness, you see,
particularly
the freshness.

The rain just gone
the gravel dry
enough to walk on,
and the sun, the sun.

Each year it gets harder
each year to wander
drinking the freshness
back to the bone.

Each year to wonder
if the gates of the garden
after the winter
open again.

Life

He had used the knife
in self-defence, to give
him something to fight about,

a grip of his life. And quick –
no argument – it struck
black from white, laid out

that shadowing past
cleancut at his feet. Tonight
he had at last

distinguished himself,
destroyed the illusion
of somebody else.

Could walk away upright.
Not he grappling alone
helpless upon the pavement.

Exact Fare Please

A great scutter,
coming on rain
just as it's dark.

Pavements chromatic,
all that brilliance
expounding the gutter.

Luminously
one by one
buses nose in,

destinations
dramatic
above the welter,

offering sure
transitory
golden shelter

numerate,
allocated,
pay-as-you-enter,

and out again
crammed to the last
splashed red light;

maybe a spit,
a final despatch,
as the doors closing.

When they are gone the dark and the rain
move in with their own
minor conclusion.

First Frost

The first frost.
Before they put down
salt and sand

grit they call it
all over town
wherever they tread

to go safe,
not skid,
to make it wet,

black enough;
you can confide
in the rough.

Not in this glass,
sheer innocence
between kerbstones

offering so natural
a fall.
Do not step off

think of the smash
imagine the loss
consider your bones,

never cross
a road like this
unless the ice

has been replaced,
do not trust
any city

off its guard,
that does not grit
every street

against invasion
by the outside season. That
is its reason. This

is the first frost, quite hard,
but in the sun –
what a pity –

so soon gone
the children never made
a decent slide.

Cold Room

I work in a Cold Room.
That is why
I wear a woolly jersey
under my white
coat. I separate

complicated
closely-related
biological molecules one from another, persuade them
up and down
long distraction of columns, they will abandon

the warmest connections.
I keep them ice-cold.
Unless chilled
they are nervous, suspicious.
They would shake themselves to pieces.

When pure
I put them in store
much colder. No
not Absolute Zero –
that's for the physicists – this would be

only, say,
minus fifty-three, a mere
Siberian winter – remember,
I deal with Life. One soon
grows used to a Cold Room, it does settle in,

bring home its own
kind of a love
if you think about it enough. As for me
I wear a woolly jersey.
Spend every Sunday evening with my wife.

Craigie Park

All these leaves
scarlet and crimson
on the grass

wet grass; Berberis,
Cotoneaster, the more talented
hybrid rowans, have shed them

it being autumn
and the time
to lay things down.

And to light up
doorways, windows
early, draw across

curtains brightly
at every room;
so many colours

springing about us, a necklace, a nightly
clasping of welcome
as we reach home.

Street after street, and almost too late.
A ring round the heart
fastening tight

as leaves go out
and the grass gutters
to a dark centre without stars.

Exit

The trees went out
one by one
then the grass, only the lichen

remained, food of the dead
reindeer, that used to
welcome it out of the snow.

Bulletin

The glaciers have come down,
dead white
at the end of the street. All over town

cold mist of their breath,
and along gutters
water runs

freezing beneath. But
the machines are out, lined up,
beautiful, their great lights

tossing back darkness. And the engineers
have promised to save us,
they have left their seats

for a last meal, when they return
all will be well, under control,
it is their skill, listen –

already upstairs
they are teaching their children
to sing like the ice.

On Passing

No it is not repeat
repeat, it is once
only and enough.

These juniper berries bunched,
sun-bosomed through the frost-
needles in the bright

snow-light, meet their first
chance to last next
spring, and no more;

rounded-off tough
sky-blue bloomed, their green
one-year behind

successors crowding about them.
It is enough
to have seen a stiff

laden juniper branch,
pausing as you are
passing, just now once

out of the snow and never,
coming back how often,
to see it this way again.

The prize the primacy of it
the instantaneous thousand
cold needles ever

afire and berries
thrusting their one spring
aware out of the cluster.

G.F. Dutton was born in 1924 of Anglo-Scottish parentage on the border of Wales. He has spent most of his life in Scotland, whose passionate austerities, urban or otherwise, edge much of his poetry.

His compulsion to explore the environment – inner and outer – accounts for his poetry. It has also driven him to be among other things a climber and ski-mountaineer (his hilarious classic, *The Ridiculous Mountains*, has recently been reprinted by Hodder), a solo wild-water swimmer (*Swimming Free*, published by Heinemann and St Martin's, but now out of print) and an internationally honoured scientist.

He has visited much of the globe from a dual Scottish base – two rooms in an industrial city street, and a wooden house among boulders and batter of wind in the eastern Highlands – where 30 years' wrestle with those particular physical metaphors engendered what has become known as a 'Marginal Garden'.

His previous books of poems, *Camp One* (M. Macdonald, 1978) and *Squaring the Waves* (Bloodaxe Books, 1986) won prizes from the Scottish Arts Council. *The Concrete Garden* (Bloodaxe Books, 1991) is a Poetry Book Society Recommendation.